Health and Family Life For Primary Schools Grade 5

Cynthia O. Smith

All Rights Reserved. No part of this publication may be reproduced, stored in a retrieval system, or transmitted, in any form or by any means, electronic, mechanical, photocopying, recording or otherwise, without the prior permission in writing of the author and publisher.

The author and publisher are still awaiting a response from some copyright owners and will acknowledge permission at the first opportunity.

Table of Contents

Self and Interpersonal Relationships
Exploring your Gifts..4
Learning About HIV and AIDS..6
Technology in our lives...8
Living Healthy..10
Knowing about drugs..12

Sexuality and Sexual Health
What's happening to my body?..14
What's happening to my body? II..16
Harassment and Bullying...18
HIV and AIDS..20

Nutrition and Physical Activity
Your Health and You...22
Keeping Healthy...24

Managing the Environment
Natural Disasters..26

Work Cited...29

THEME: Self and Interpersonal Relationships

Lesson: 1

Exploring your Gifts

Gifts are the natural talents, abilities, or qualities one possesses. All gifts come from God. All of them have a purpose.

Some people have the gift of intelligence, performing or public speaking. Others have athletic abilities. Some individuals have the gift of a funny personality, while others are easy-going and wonderful to talk to.

Every person has one kind of gift or another, which is important to his or her growth and development and building positive self-esteem.

Individuals can use their gifts to make a difference in their homes, at school and in the community.

Individuals can also develop their gifts by choosing to participate in activities that require their special abilities.

Date: _____

Design a poster representing the hobbies or things you enjoy doing.

Lesson: 2

Learning About HIV and AIDS

People living with or affected by HIV and AIDS (PLWHA) need acceptance, support and understanding, just as with any other life-threatening illness.

Always demonstrate appropriate behaviours when interacting with PLWHA.

- Show compassion by being a friend to the person;
- Remember, casual contact (a hug, a handshake, or a kiss on the check) poses no threat of infection to anyone.
- Treat them as valuable human beings - as you would treat everyone else.
- Practice healthy habits/ Universal Precaution to protect you and others.
- Do not discriminate against them or make them feel worse.
- Do not blame anyone who has contracted HIV virus.
- Never share information about a person's health status without their permission.

Activity
Creative writing: Write a story about a person who is affected with an illness (Include appropriate and inappropriate behaviours).

Date: _____

1. Complete the information how AIDs is not spread.

1. by _____

2. _____ such as mosquitoes

3. Using the _____

4. by _____ blood

5. _____ hands

2. Complete the information how AIDs is spread.
3.

6. By _____ sex.

7. Using contaminated _____

8. From _____ to baby

7

Lesson: 3

Technology in our lives

Technology is the application of tools and methods of applying technical knowledge.

Technology has always impacted human life, but today's children live in a world in which technology is changing very quickly and affecting so many areas of their lives e.g.
Education: computers, internet, TV, radio, video, CD and DVD players, etc
Communication: cell phones, telephones, computers, text messages, iPods, etc.
Entertainment: TV, radio, video, CD and DVD players, etc.
Family Living: appliances, equipment, automobiles, etc.

While no technology is good or bad in and of itself, every new technology poses moral choices. How technology is used can have a positive or negative effect on one's development.

Children need to make healthy decisions about whether to use these technologies in ways that will help them grow and develop into healthy, productive citizens

Guidelines for Safe Use of Technology:
- Balance the time spent in using technology with wholesome activities, e.g. reading, gardening, sports, etc.
- Exercise common sense to evaluate products advertised on the internet
- Avoid talking to people who they don't know in chat rooms or on the internet
- Use the internet for constructive purposes instead of surfing the net
- Exercise precaution when viewing various technology devices, e.g. imitating what athletes and superstars in magazines and on TV do. These actions can result in unhealthy behaviours and can harm the body.
-Internet usage can expose you to identity theft, abductions, rape or death.

Compare technology used today in the past.

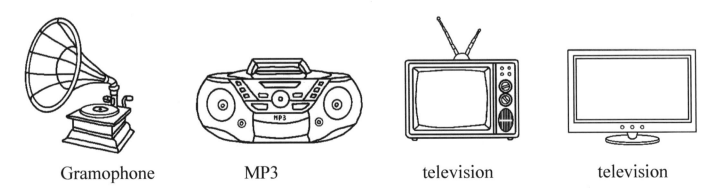

Gramophone   MP3   television   television

Date: _____

1. Compile a list of new technologies that you have experienced in your lifetime.

_____   _____
_____   _____
_____   _____

2. Define the term technology.

_____
_____

3. Write the correct name for each device

| iphone | ipad-mp3 | camera | flip phone | laptop | camera |

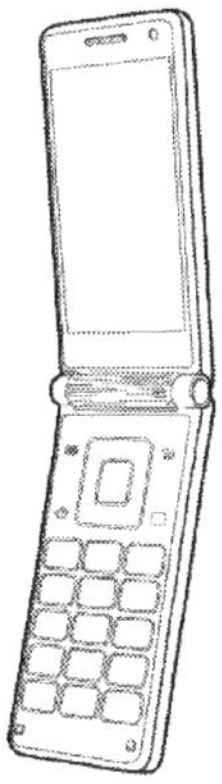

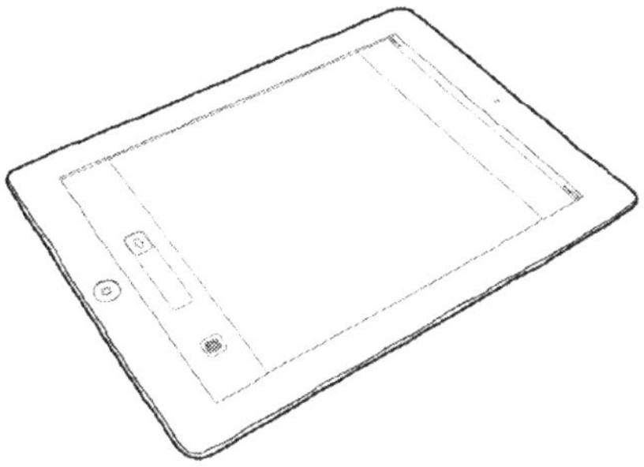

Lesson: 4

Living Healthy

Wellness is defined as a state of good health (physical, social, emotional and intellectual development).

As you get older, it becomes more important for you to take responsibility for your wellness. Practicing healthy habits contributes to wellness and promotes a positive self-image.

Health habits that contribute to wellness:
- Exercise regularly to keep the body fit
- Eat healthy foods and drink water daily
- Get at least eight to ten hours sleep every night
- Keep your body, hair, nails and teeth clean
- Visit the doctor and dentist for regular check-ups
- Wash your hands often, especially before eating and after using the restroom.
- Wear safety gear to protect the body from injury

There are community clinics and Government and Non-Government Agencies that provide services and information to promote wellness.

Date: _____

Write the letter from each picture next to the word. Put an X on the unhealthy choices.

Drink alcohol ____

Bathe ____

Eat fruits ____

Eat sweets ____

Drink water ____

Drink beer ____

Smoke marijuana ____

Eat grains and nuts ____

Smoke cigarette ____

Get rest ____

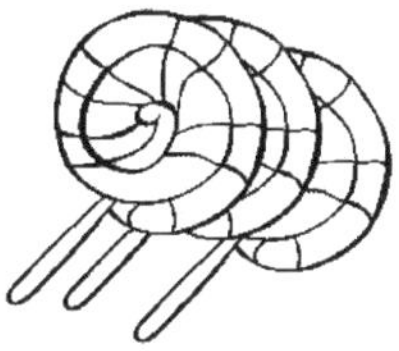

11

Lesson: 5

Knowing about drugs

Drugs cover substances such as medicine, cocaine, marijuana, heroin, ecstasy, tobacco and alcohol. Medicines are drugs that cause helpful changes in the body when used correctly.

Illegal drugs contain various chemicals. Most give some sort of pleasure. The use of illegal drugs has serious effects on a person's life. These drugs can be habit-forming or lead to addiction. Even legal drug such as alcohol and tobacco tend to be habit-forming.

Addiction is a constant need for something that leads to habitual use. Users of illegal drugs often become drug addicts.

Reasons to refuse drugs:
- Drugs are unhealthful and can harm your body
- Use of drugs is against the law
- Drugs destroy relationships with friends and family
- Drugs keep you from doing well in school and achieving your goals

Refusing drugs is one of the most healthful decisions you can make. It helps you build self-respect. Saying no to drugs helps you keep your mind clear.

How to avoid drug use and abuse:
Say no, and tell why not
Repeat no and walk away
Suggest something else to do
Avoid pressure to use drugs, commit crime or violence
Go to places where drugs are not used
Have friends who don't do drugs
If you have a problem, talk with your parents or other trusted adults

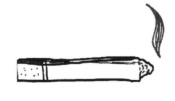

marijuana cocaine tobacco alcohol.

Date: _____

1. Complete a KWL Chart on Illegal Drugs. Research the most commonly abused drugs in The Bahamas.

What Drugs We know	What We want to Learn About Drugs	What We Learned From Our Investigation

2. Look at the two pictures, then write the consequences of drugs.

A
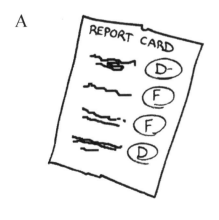

B

_____
_____
_____

THEME: Sexuality and Sexual Health

Lesson: 6

What's happening to my body?

All human beings grow and develop in a given sequence but at different rates.

Puberty is the period during adolescence when the body begins to develop and change. Puberty usually starts between ages 8 and 13 in girls and 10 and 15 in boys. Everyone begins puberty at his or her own pace.

During puberty, male and female hormones are released into the bloodstream. Hormones are chemicals that cause body growth and physical, emotional and mental changes.

Physical Changes and Development:
Physical changes during puberty affect the way the body looks. These changes can be dramatic and disturbing
- Oily skin/acne
- Sudden growth
- Sometimes clumsy
- Increased perspiration and body odour.

Physical Changes in Boys	Physical Changes in Girls
- Shoulders broaden	- Breasts develop
- Muscles grow	- Hips broaden
- Hair grows under arms, on arms, legs, chest and face; and around penis and testicles (pubic area)	- Hair grows on pubic areas (under arms and around vulva and vagina)
- Penis, testes and scrotum grow larger	- Vagina, vulva and clitoris grow slightly
- Voice gets deeper	- Vagina discharges white, sticky substance, the vagina's way of cleaning itself, which is normal
- Wet dream	- Menstruation begins

Mental growth occurs as teens learn to examine consequences and plan for the future.

Mental changes and development:
- Attention span increases
- Ability to think and solve problems
- Develop new interests

Activity

Use a diagram. Label where changes occur on male and female diagrams.

Date: _____

Many changes will happen to boys and girls during puberty. Some change are unique to boys and some are unique to girls. Some change happen to both. Can you tick the correct box for the changes below?

	Boys	Girls	Both
Grow pubic hair			
Get taller			
Start periods			
Get erections			
Feet grow			
Sweat more			
Grow breast			
Grow facial hair			
Testicles grow			
Voice gets deeper			
Penis grows			
Get wet dreams			
Hips get wider			
Shoulders get wider			
Get smellier			
Produce eggs			
Produce sperm			

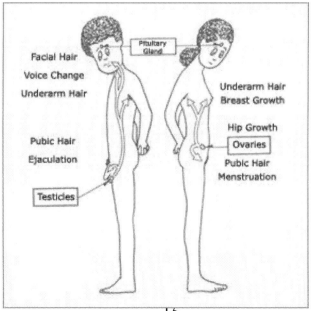

Lesson: 7

What's happening to my body? II

Emotional Changes and Development:
- Self-consciousness about body changes
- Mood swings from happiness to sadness
- Developing friendships with the opposite sex
- Awkwardness and shyness

Emotional growth requires controlling and dealing with emotions appropriately.

Coping with Changes during Puberty:
Puberty begins at different times for different people. Being able to cope with the changes is important for a healthy body, mind and spirit.
- Take care of your body and practice good personal hygiene, e.g. Wash and dry the sexual organs thoroughly, use a deodorant or baking soda under arms to control odour,
- wash your hair at least every two weeks (boys more often)
- Pursue and develop skills in activities that interest you
- Engage in activities to manage stress, e.g. reading, listening to music, volunteering or helping others, etc.

Activity
Write an essay on what students can do to maintain good hygiene and how girls can keep their bodies healthy during menstruation.

Date: _____

When boys reach puberty their voice_____
They will start to grow _____on their face, around their penis and testicles, and under their _____.
A boy penis and testicles will _____. They might start to have _____.

When girls reach puberty their breast_____
They will start to grow _____under their arms, and around their pubic area. Their hips will _____. They might have _____ and _____ hair.
They will start their _____.

Lesson: 8

Harassment and Bullying

Harassment is any form of repeated attention that is not wanted and affects your ability to do your schoolwork or to live your life peacefully.

Harassment can be physical or verbal. It can occur in the form of bullying or sexual harassment.

Bullying is the picking on people who are alone or who seem different in some way. Forms of Bullying are: Spreading rumours, excluding others, name-calling, fighting, and threatening (verbal, text and email threats).

Impact of harassment/bullying:
- Change in behaviour (withdrawn/ill-tempered)
- Change in social life (not seeing friends or staying away from clubs)
- Feeling of anger, hurt and fear
- Eating disorder, depression and low self-esteem
- Suicide

Date: _____

1. List FOUR things you can do to avoid getting into a fight with a bully.

_____
_____
_____
_____

2. Look at the pictures below. Write the description that correctly matches each picture.

| hitting | cyber internet bullying | kicking | yelling |

_____   _____

_____   _____

Lesson: 9

HIV and AIDS

HIV is a virus which stands for (Human Immune-deficiency Virus). When this virus attacks the immune system, it makes it weak and unable to protect against infections and diseases.

HIV is different from most of the other communicable diseases because it is an STI and requires contact with body fluids such as blood, saliva, urine, etc. It has no cure or vaccine to prevent it.

Transmission of HIV:
HIV is carried by body fluids such as blood, semen, vaginal fluids and breast milk of an infected person. It is generally passed on through:
- Unprotected sexual intercourse;
- Blood transfusion / Sharing needles;
- An infected woman to her baby during birth, or through breastfeeding

Non-transmission of HIV:
The HIV virus does not pass through the air. You cannot get it from being in the same room with an infected person.
You cannot get it by touching or hugging, sharing pencils or hairbrushes or even food. The HIV virus causes AIDS which stands for **Acquired Immune Deficiency Syndrome**. People with AIDS die from other diseases they get such as pneumonia and cancer.

Prevention of HIV and AIDS:
Make choices that keep you healthy
- Abstain from sex until you are an adult or married
- Never use drugs. They impair your judgment
- Have one faithful sexual partner

Treatment of HIV and AIDS:
To date, there is no cure for HIV. Scientists have developed drugs to treat HIV infection. Drug treatment improves the survival time for patients.

Caring for Persons Affected by HIV and AIDS
- People who are HIV positive should be treated like everyone else, with respect and dignity.
- Get factual information about the disease.
- Show kindness, love and support for persons living with and affected by HIV and AIDS.'
- Do not spread gossip or discriminate against them.

Date: _____

1. Explain what HIV is.

_____

_____

2. What does the acronym AIDS stands for?

_____

_____

3. Create a chart listing how HIV and AIDS is transmitted and not transmitted

Ways HIV is transmitted

_____
_____
_____
_____
_____
_____
_____
_____

Ways HIV is not transmitted

_____
_____
_____
_____
_____
_____
_____
_____
_____
_____

THEME: Nutrition and Physical Activity

Lesson: 10

Your Health and You

Maintaining a healthy lifestyle involves balancing food intake with physical activity.

Many diseases that lead to death are directly related to lifestyle choices, e.g. poor eating or drinking habits, lack of exercise, drug use, etc.

Persons who are overweight or obese (very fat) are at higher risk or more likely to develop lifestyle diseases.

Lifestyle diseases such as heart disease, diabetes, hypertension (high blood pressure), cancer and AIDS are the leading causes of death in The Bahamas.

These diseases can be prevented with better lifestyle choices:
- Practice healthy eating by making healthy food choices
- Exercise regularly
- Get enough sleep every night
- Avoid using drugs such as alcohol, tobacco, marijuana, etc.

Foods in the Food Guide Drum and Dietary Guidelines are grouped according to type.*

Following the dietary guidelines will help individuals stay healthy and reduce the risk of chronic disease, e.g. diabetes, heart disease and high blood pressure and obesity.

Meals usually contain more than one type of food, e.g. salads, sandwiches, pizza, etc. These are called combination foods.

Tips for choosing combination meals:
- When choosing combination foods, use the food guidelines to determine the food groups identified in each menu choice.
- Examine the menu and determine if the selected foods are or include foods from a variety of food groups.
- If necessary, revise menu choice to include foods from a variety of food groups.

Date: _____

1. Identify FOUR common life style diseases in The Bahamas.

_____   _____

_____   _____

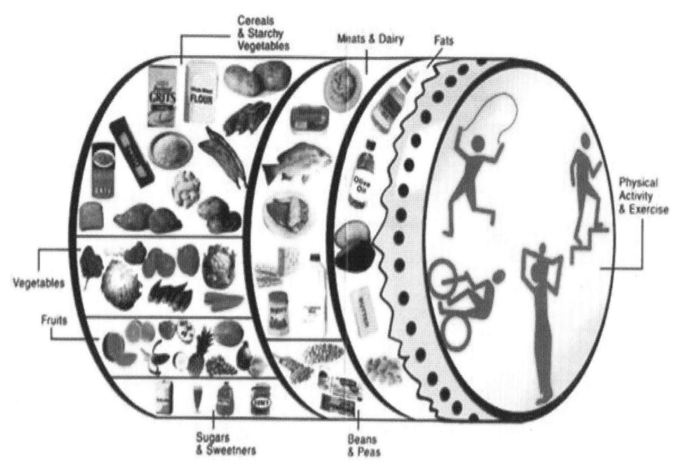

2. Use the Food Drum to list the following.

Two vegetables: _____ _____

Two fruits: _____ _____

Two sugar & Sweeteners: _____ _____

Two Beans & peas _____ _____

Two Meats & dairy _____ _____

Two Fat _____ _____

Cereal and Starchy Vegetables _____

_____

Lesson: 11

Keeping Healthy

Daily physical activity is part of a healthy lifestyle. Regular physical activity helps to keep the body healthy.

Benefits of regular physical activity:
- Good posture and a leaner and attractive body
- Stronger muscles and bones
- Good self-image/self-worth
- Increases endurance
- Improves cardiovascular fitness and helps maintain a healthy weight
- Reduces risks of contracting heart diseases and cancer
- Helps lower blood pressure
- Improves sleep and relaxation

Children who are engaged in regular physical activities look and feel better. It also improves their cognitive development. (Children who balance physical activity with good health practices and learning, do better in school).

Areas of focus and recommended physical activity: - Improving flexibility
- Cardiovascular fitness
- Muscular strength
- Endurance

Tips for engaging in physical activities:
- Determine what area of fitness you need to work on and plan your personal exercise programme
- Keep safety in mind
- Set goals for your fitness programme
- Warm up before working out and cool off after a workout.

Activity

Design an Activity Drum Guide of the physical activities that they can engage in everyday to stay healthy.

Date: _____

1. Compile of list of safety rules to follow when engaging in physical activities.

2. List SIX benefits of the regular physical activity.

THEME: Managing the Environment

Lesson: 12

Natural Disasters

Any natural event that causes widespread injury, death and property damage is known as a natural disaster, e.g. hurricane, storm, tornado, flood, earthquake, and Tsunami.

Every year hurricanes, storms, tornadoes and floods occur in The Bahamas. Knowing what to do during these natural disasters could mean the difference between life and death.

A **hurricane** is a storm that forms over tropical areas of oceans and can move inland. In a hurricane, rain is heavy, and winds blow greater than 75 miles per hour.

A **tropical storm** also forms over tropical areas of oceans. Wind speeds vary between 40 and 75 miles per hour.

A **tornado** is a violently rotating funnel-shaped column of air associated with a thunderstorm. Signs such as dark greenish sky, large hail and a loud roar occur. Tornadoes can form quickly without warning.

Hurricanes and thunderstorms can cause major flooding, especially in low-lying areas.

In The Bahamas, the hurricane season runs from June through November.

A **hurricane watch** means hurricane conditions are possible within 36 hours. A **hurricane warning** means hurricane conditions are expected within 24 hours.

Safety During Hurricanes and Tropical Storms
- If you live or visit hurricane prone areas, be sure to prepare an evacuation plan before watches or warnings.
- If a hurricane watch or warning has been issued, bring indoors all outdoor items that could be blown by the wind.
- If a hurricane warning has been issued, listen to the radio or television for evacuation instructions.
- Close hurricane shutters or board windows from outside with plywood. If you do not have to evacuate, stay indoors and away from windows.
- Persons who live in low-lying areas or near seas should go to a **Hurricane Shelter** identified in their community.

The National Emergency Management Agency (NEMA) is responsible for the overall management of natural disasters in The Bahamas. NEMA works with Government and Non- Government Agencies such as the Royal Bahamas Defense Force, the Royal Bahamas Police Force, the Department of Meteorology, the Broadcasting Corporation of The Bahamas and other media houses and The Bahamas Red Cross Society to manage natural disasters in The Bahamas

Items Needed During Any Natural Disaster
- Weather radio or other battery-powered radio or television
- Battery-powered lights and flashlights
- Candles, dry matches and extra batteries
- A gallon of water per person for at least 3 days
- Medicines family members might need
- Blankets and/or sleeping bags
- Soap, hygiene supplies and a first aid kit (It is important to check a first aid kit at least every three months to replace any items that were used.)
- Canned or packaged foods that don't need to be refrigerated or cooked. – enough for several days, manual can opener, eating utensils

Date: _____

1. Identify the natural disasters that occur on your island.

_____   _____

2. Describe natural disasters and their effects on families and communities.

_____

_____

3. Identify SIX agencies that respond to natural disasters.

_____

_____

_____

_____

_____

4. Identify the natural disasters below. Write the names on the line

| hurricane | tornado | earthquake |

_____   _____

_____

Work Cited

Commonwealth of The Bahamas Ministry of Education Primary Health and Family Life Education Curriculum Guidelines Grades 4 -6, 2012

Darville, J. Bahamian Food Drum

Credit is given to the following graphics and fonts

Made in the USA
Las Vegas, NV
22 June 2023